THE ATHEIST COLORING AND ACTIVITY BOOK

This book was intended for adult Atheists. Others are advised to use reader discretion.

written by John Simons

illustrated by Chelsea Webb

colored by _____
(print your name here)

Copyright John Simons 2014
ISBN 978-0-615-98477-3
Quotations from the Authorized Version (King James) Bible

NEXT BIG THING BOOKS
7095 Hollywood Blvd.
Los Angeles, CA 90028

Contents

1. Who Are the Atheists?
2. Are Atheists Spiritual People?
3. We Are Born Atheists.
4. Serenity
5. A Just and Peaceful World
6. Wars and Gods
7. Our Extinct Cousins
8. Religion Treats Women Badly.
9. Joan of Arc
10. Do We Depend Upon God and the Bible for Our Morality?
11. Absolute Morality
12. Adam Receiving Original Sin from God
13. The Creation of Guilt
14. The Creation of Atheism
15. Finding Answers
16. The Biological Purpose of Life
17. The Personal Purpose of Life
18. The Purpose of Sex
19. Saint Augustine's Dilemma
20. The Source of Original Sin
21. Saint Monica
22. Know the Truth.
23. Cogito Ergo Atheos Sum.
24. Close to God
25. Always Out of Reach
26. Martin Luther
27. Henry III
28. Starting Life
29. God and Devil
30. Good and Evil
31. One God
32. Power vs. Knowledge
33. The Ontological Argument
34. The Road to Rationality
35. Heaven or Hell
36. Keeping the Faith
37. The Great Commission
38. Religious Logic
39. Answering Prayer
40. Why the Gospels Were Written
41. Why a Coloring Book?
42. Why Convert the World?
43. This Generation
44. The Body of Christ
45. Temptation
46. Changed Names
47. The Standard Jesus
48. Studying Biology
49. When the Old Testament Bible Got It Right!
50. Free-will Choices
51. Pie in the Sky
52. Off the Hook
53. God's Good Deed
54. Why Everything Exists
55. Arguing Back
56. Not Much New Under the Sun
57. The Eleven Commandments
58. How Do We Explain Everything? Number 1
59. How Do We Explain Everything? Number 2
60. What Caused the Big Bang?
61. Some "First Cause" Must Have Created the Big Bang.
62. Thermodynamics
63. Randomness (Entropy) Increases Over Time
64. Open System
65. The End
66. Activity: Atheist On Board
67. Activity: Feed the Hungry.
68. Make a Mobile part 1: Triple Trouble
69. Make a Mobile part 2: Shining Stars
70. Activity: Change the Pledge.
71. Activity: BLAH, BLAH, BLAH
72. Activity: Get Involved.

Who Are the Atheists?

They are the:
nonbelievers
agnostics
undecided
unchurched
secularists
rationalists
materialists
free-thinkers
humanists
decline to state
none of the above
wait and see
etc.

As they do not profess faith in a god, they are by definition Atheists.
Could they be an unrecognized majority?

Are Atheists Spiritual People?

Of course we are!

The highest level of our consciousness makes us appreciate nature and the beautiful things that our fellow humans have created.

We Are Born Atheists.

Babies come into this world as Atheists.
They bring no knowledge of any gods.

Diseases such as Alzheimer's can leave one as innocent of religion at the end of life as at birth.

Serenity

To find serenity in life we must make peace with ourselves, not with some supernatural god.

A Just and Peaceful World

Making a just and peaceful world is the responsibility of each and every one of us. No god will do it for us.

Wars and Gods

Endlessly fighting wars against our neighbors and worshipping supernatural gods are primitive and uncivilized relics of our past.

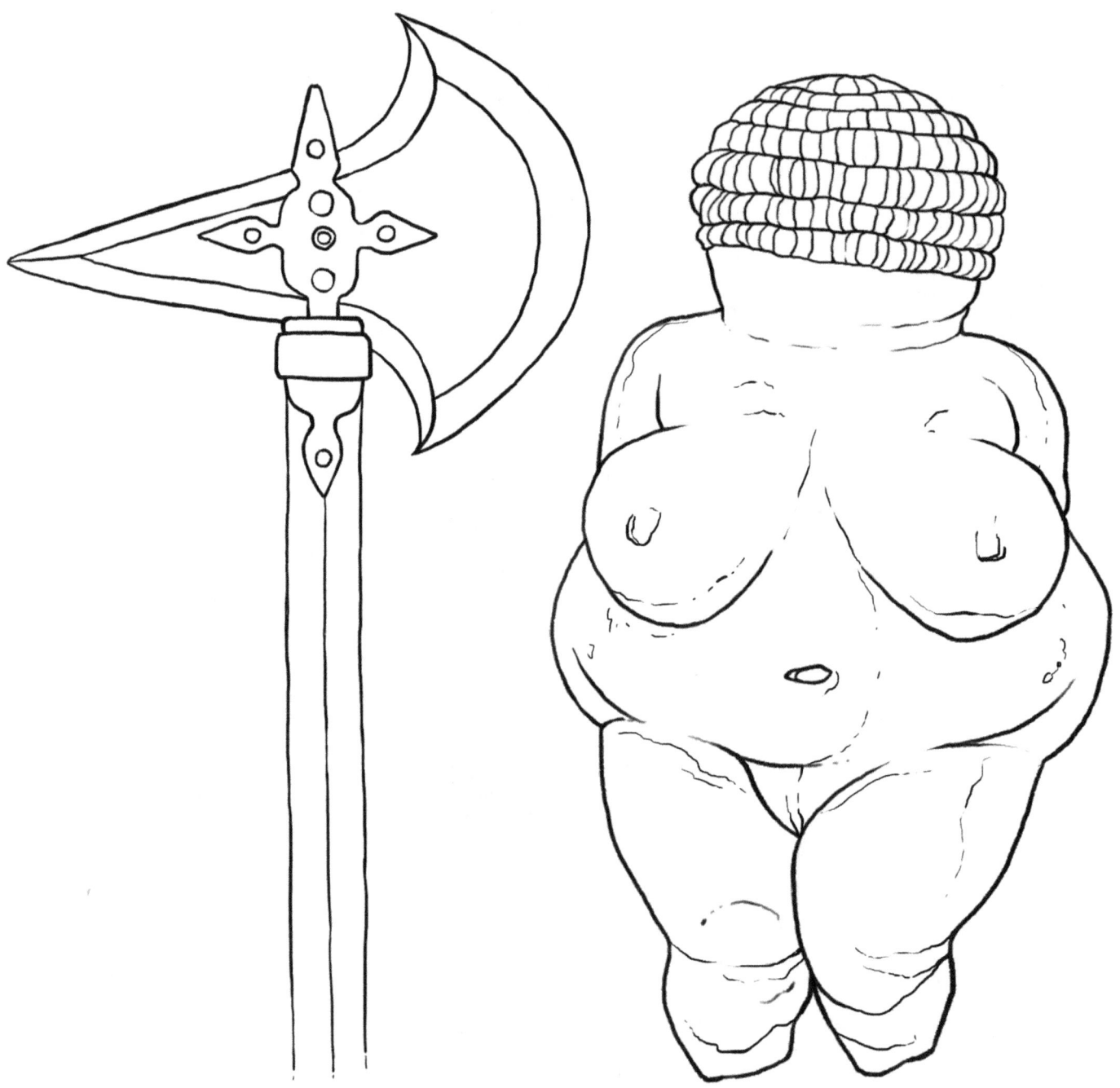

These behaviors should be discouraged rather than honored and rewarded.

Our Extinct Cousins

At least two different species of human beings once lived at the same time in Europe.

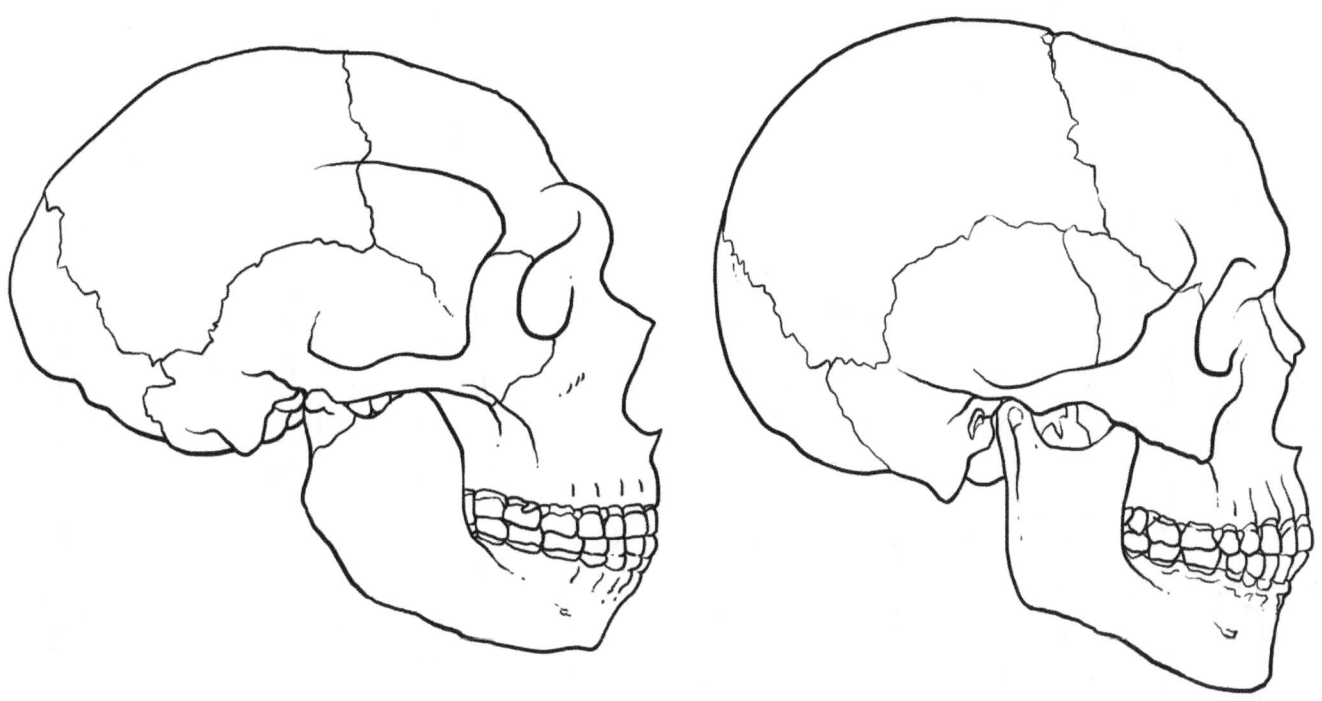

Homo neanderthalensis   Homo sapiens

Only the more aggressive and warlike species survived.

Religion Treats Women Badly.

It tries to make them either virgin queens or completely invisible.

Joan of Arc

Joan of Arc (ca. 1412-1431) was told by God in a vision to free her country from its enemies. After winning battles she was captured and burned at the stake at age 19.

She was declared a saint in 1920, the same year that American women won the right to vote. The church took 489 years to realize that this dynamic and capable woman was a saint. Why do you think it waited so long?

Do We Depend upon God and the Bible for Our Morality?

Hardly. We have hundreds of volumes of statute law to tell us what is permitted and what is forbidden.

Absolute Morality

Teresa of Calcutta (1910-1997) believed in absolute morality: that some things always are wrong regardless of circumstances. She opposed birth control in Calcutta even though the population far outstripped the resources needed to support it.

As a result, many people suffered and died. Do you think that most Atheists would agree with Teresa?

Adam Receiving Original Sin from God

The Oedipus complex is original sin secularized.
Both concepts leave one condemned before starting out
in life.

The Creation of Guilt

Religion is all about guilt, especially guilt over sex.

The Creation of Atheism

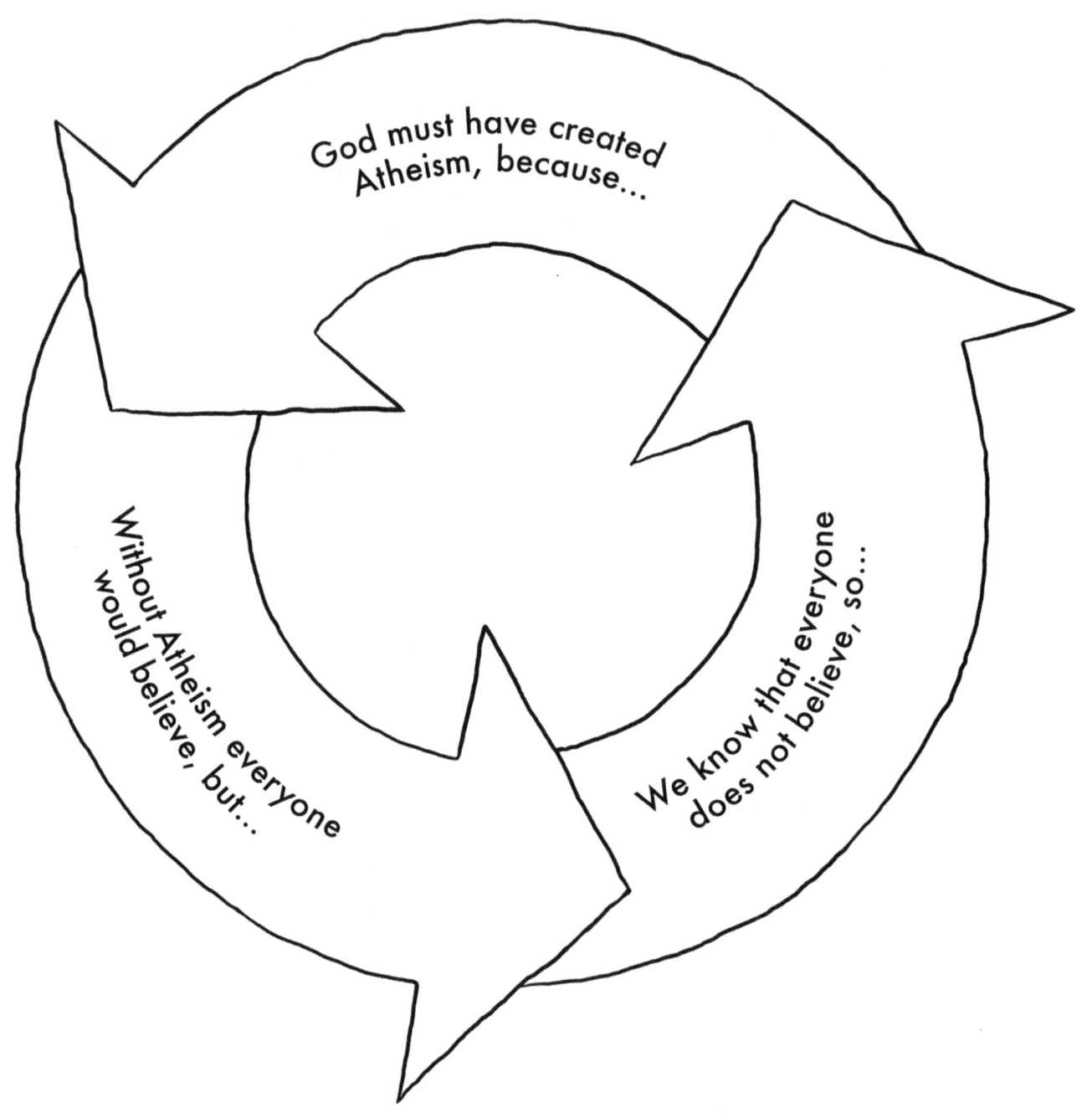

This makes sense. Right?

Finding Answers

GENESIS (the first book of the Bible) Finding an Easy Answer

*Jove refers to Jupiter

REVELATION (the last book of the Bible) There Is No Easy Answer

*a unified field theory

The Biological Purpose of Life

Nature's plan is to renew life continually.

The Personal Purpose of Life

Connect the dots to find out what people are looking for in life.

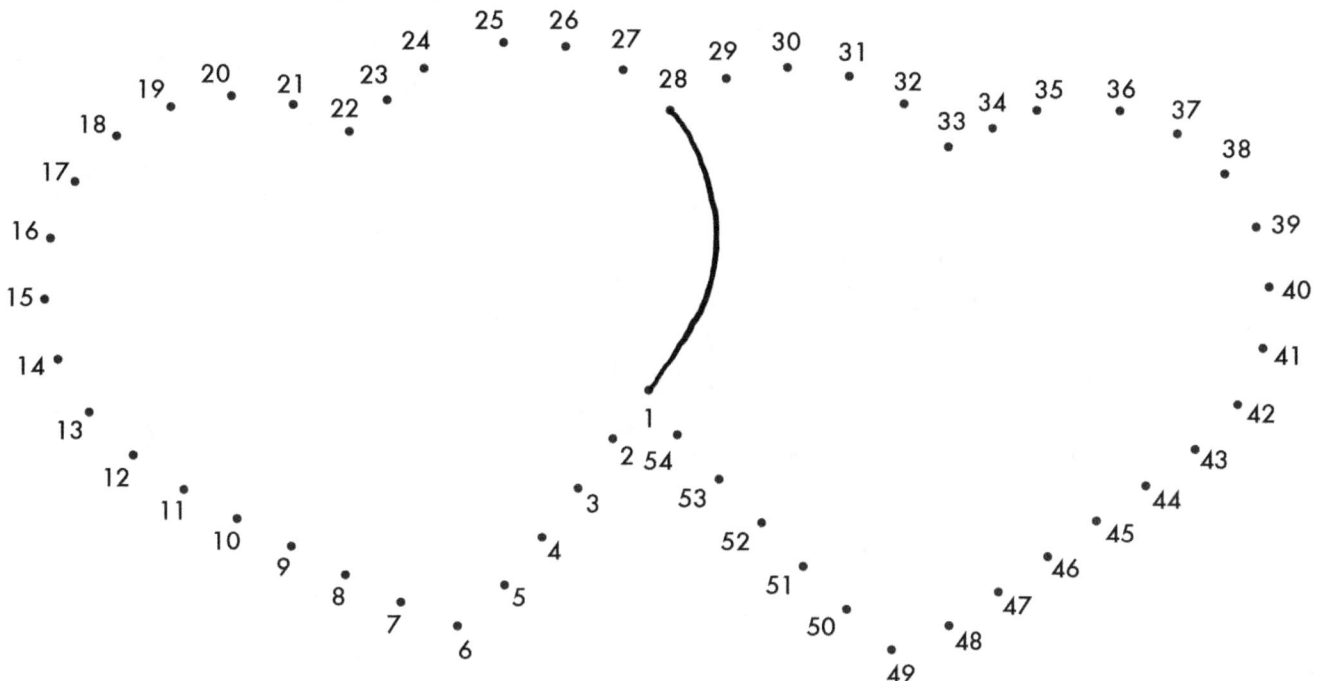

Everyone is seeking happiness. The easiest way to acheive it is by making someone else happy.

The Purpose of Sex
(in addition to making babies)

Sex keeps men close to home, as two parents were needed by our ancestors to rear the young. Thus frequent mating is completely natural and moral.

Saint Augustine's Dilemma

Saint Augustine felt that he needed to give up sex to find God, but then, he needed God's help to give up sex.

His choice: sex or salvation.
Only after his testosterone level dropped
did he accept Christianity.

The Source of Original Sin

Saint Augustine (354-430) said that the sexual pleasure of parents creates original sin in their child.

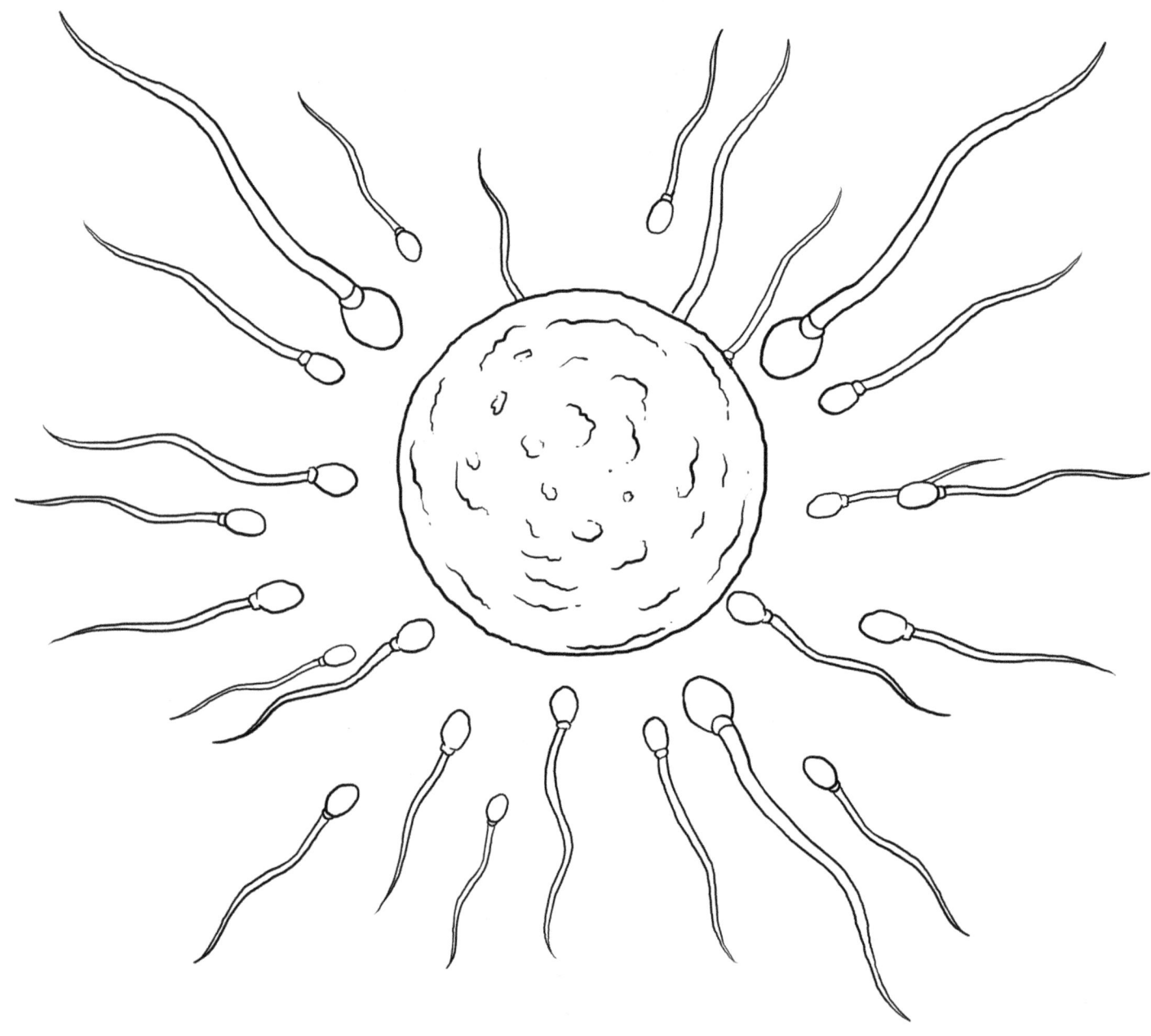

Obviously, evolution made mating pleasurable to encourage reproduction. Those who did not like sex left fewer descendants.

Saint Monica

Saint Monica (ca. 331-387) was the mother of St. Augustine and is patron of the victims of adultery. She was a Christian married to a pagan. Her husband had many infidelities, but she never complained. She said that Eve was created to be Adam's helpmate, therefore she should subordinate herself to her husband.

The church must have considered her
the ideal wife when it made her a saint.
What do you think of her?

Know the Truth.

A favorite New Testament quotation is John 8:32, "And ye shall know the truth, and the truth shall make you free."

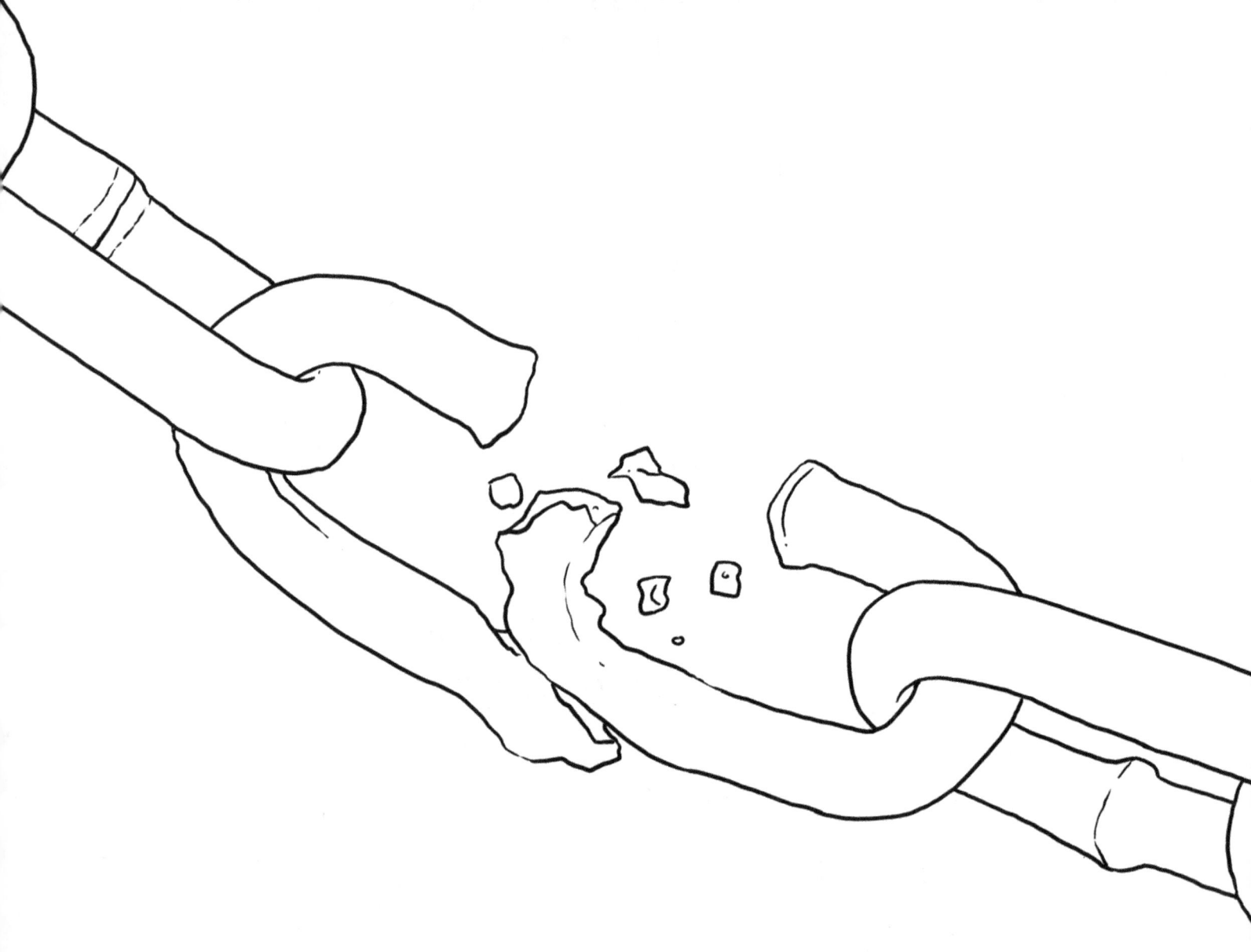

The truth is that no gods exist for us to sin against. That makes one free to think about sex without feeling like an evil person.

Cogito Ergo Atheos Sum.

How can one be both an open-minded thinker and a faithful follower?

Always Out of Reach

God lies hidden somewhere over the rainbow,
never allowing us to experience him directly.

Martin Luther

Martin Luther (1483-1546) broke the monopoly of the Roman Catholic Church when he brought western Christianity out of the Middle Ages and into the Renaissance.

The many sects that sprang up must be teaching errors as all of their varying doctrines cannot be true.

Henry VIII

Henry VIII (1491-1547) was King of England from 1509 to his death. He broke away from the Roman Catholic Church so that he could divorce his queen and remarry.

Since then divorce and contraception have become well accepted. When will a woman's right to choose an abortion also become non-controversial?

Starting Life

For a church to arrange for souls to go to heaven upon death, it must have arranged for them to come from heaven in the first place.

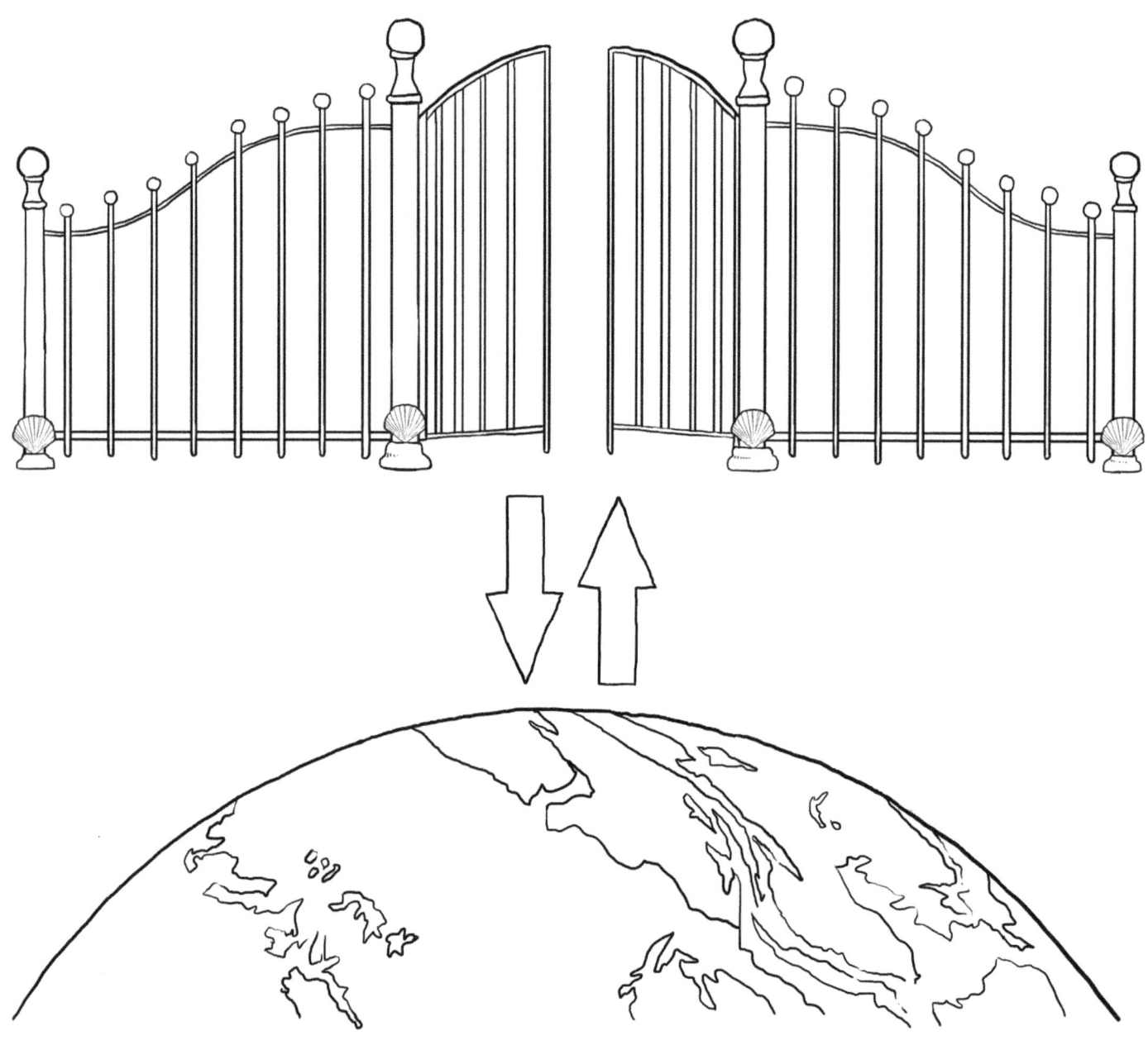

You would not expect one power without the other.
Therefore one asks: Is religion relevant to birth and death?

God and Devil

An infinitely good god and an infinitely bad devil cannot co-exist.

They would annihilate each other in a burst of energy like particles of matter and anti-matter.

Good and Evil

Because God created evil, see Isaiah 45:7, and allows it to exist, he cannot be all good.

Therefore some evil must exist in God, and logically, some good must exist in the Devil.

One God

Everything in our existence is a mixture of good and bad.
This would be a reflection of God's nature, if a god existed.

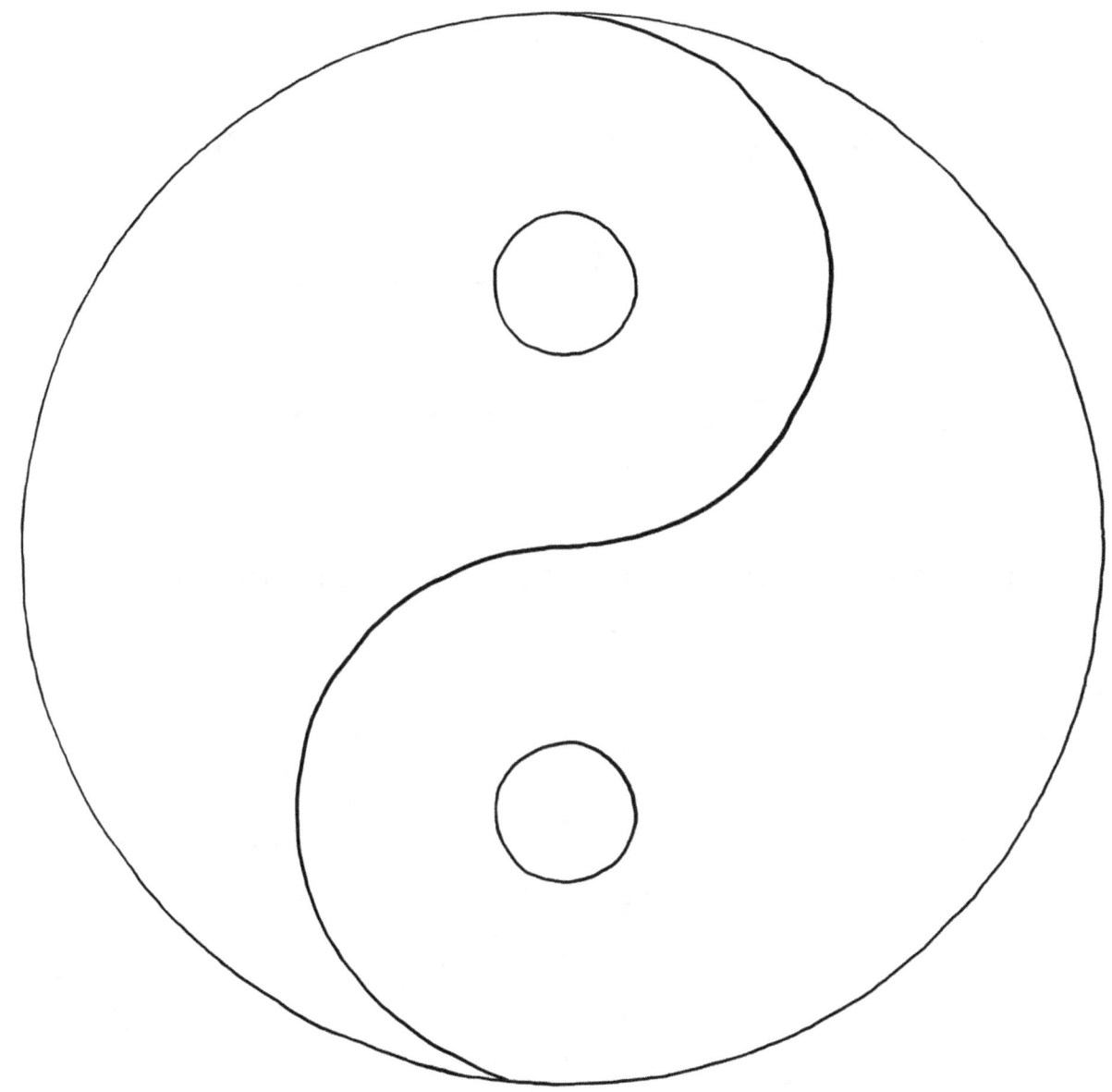

Therefore a creating god would have to be both good and bad,
or to express it differently, God and Devil would be but one deity.

Power vs. Knowledge

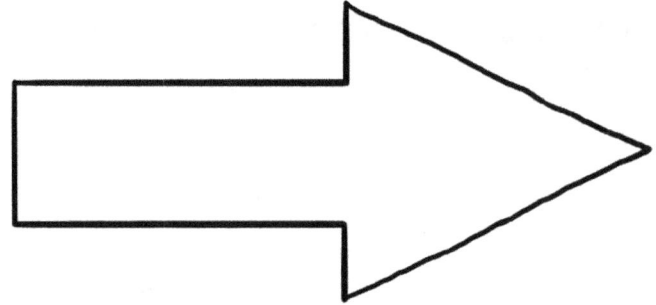

An omnipotent god can change future events.

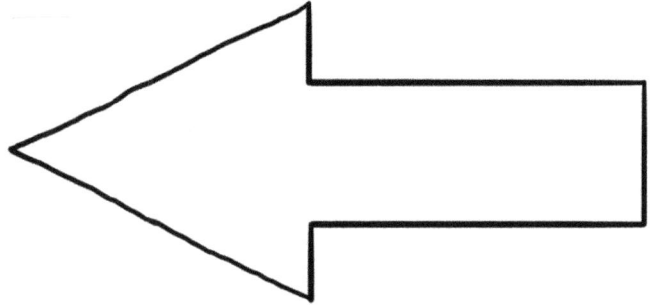

An omniscient god already knows the result of future events.

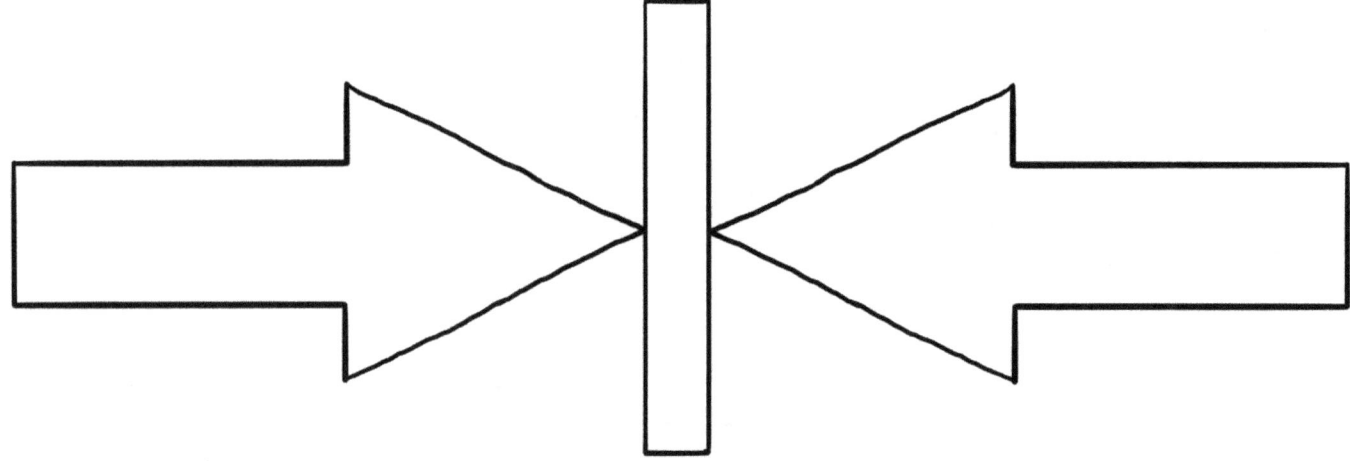

Logically, if God already knows how events will turn out he cannot change them, or he would not have known how they would turn out. Therefore, he cannot be both all-powerful and all-knowing.

The Ontological Argument

All religious arguments start by assuming, through prior faith, that a god exists.

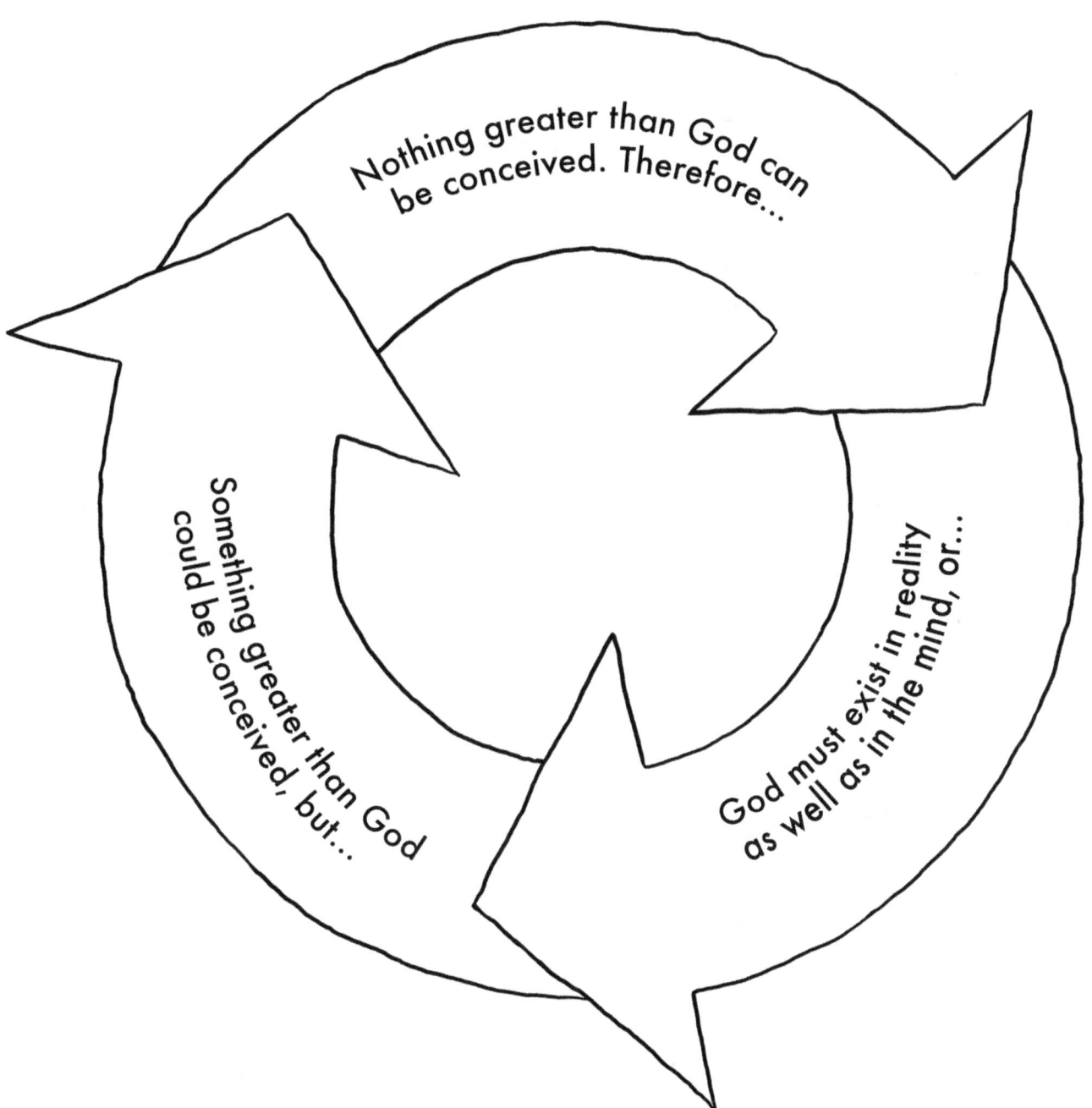

However, agnosticism recognizes that we cannot know what may lie beyond nature, making impossible any objective proof that a god either exists or does not exist.

The Road to Rationality

WARNING:
You may arrive at Enlightenment
without ever getting to Contentment.

Heaven

FOR BELIEVERS: those who do not think for themselves—
the credulous, the gullible, the naive, the religious.

Or Hell

FOR THE REST OF US: those who think for themselves—
the realists, the doubters, the questioners, the Atheists.

Is this division fair and sensible?

Keeping the Faith

Faith of our fathers, holy faith!
We will be true to thee till death.
-English Catholic hymn, 1849

The Great Commission

Christianity is not a live and let live religion.

The Great Commission, found in Matthew 28:19, states: "Go ye therefore, and teach all nations, baptizing them in the name of the Father, and of the Son, and of the Holy Ghost."

Religious Logic

Logically, something created all of this.
Logically, it must be God.
Logically, God must be infinite.
Logically, God must be immortal.
Logically, God must be all-powerful.
Logically, God must be all-knowing.
Logically, God must be all-merciful.
Logically, God must be all-loving.
Logically, God must be just.
Logically, God must hear our prayers.

Answering Prayer

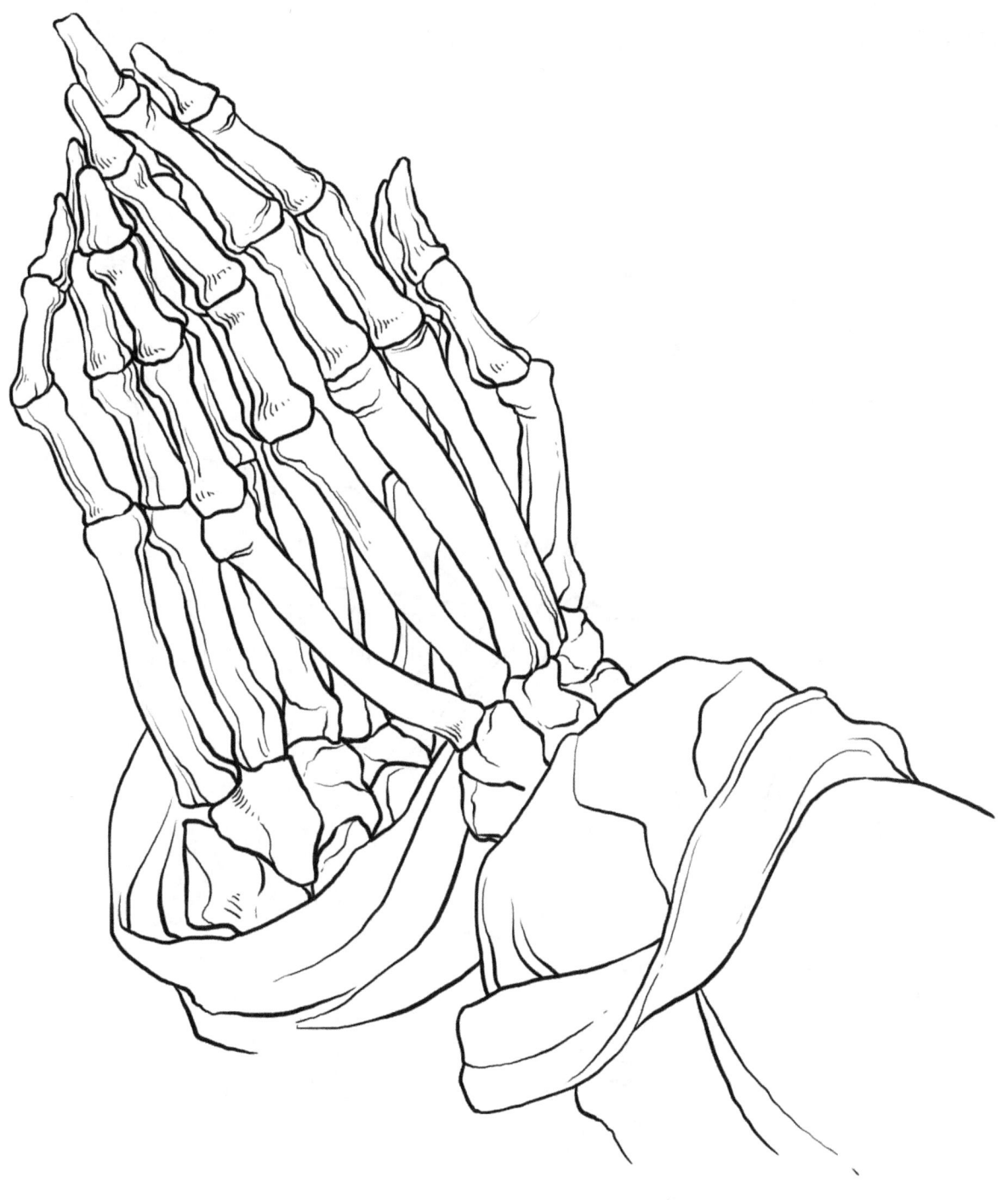

To have all your prayers granted,
pray that God's will be done.

Why the Gospels Were Written

John 20:31 says, "But these are written, that ye might believe that Jesus is the Christ, the Son of God; and that believing ye might have life through his name."

Thus the gospels were written to convince you to believe, not to record historic events.

Why a Coloring Book?

These words were written and these pictures were drawn to encourage you to think realistically about ultimate concerns.

If we did not take these matters seriously we would not have produced this coloring book.

Why Convert the World?

Matthew 24:14 says, "And this gospel of the kingdom shall be preached in all the world for a witness unto all nations; and then shall the end come."

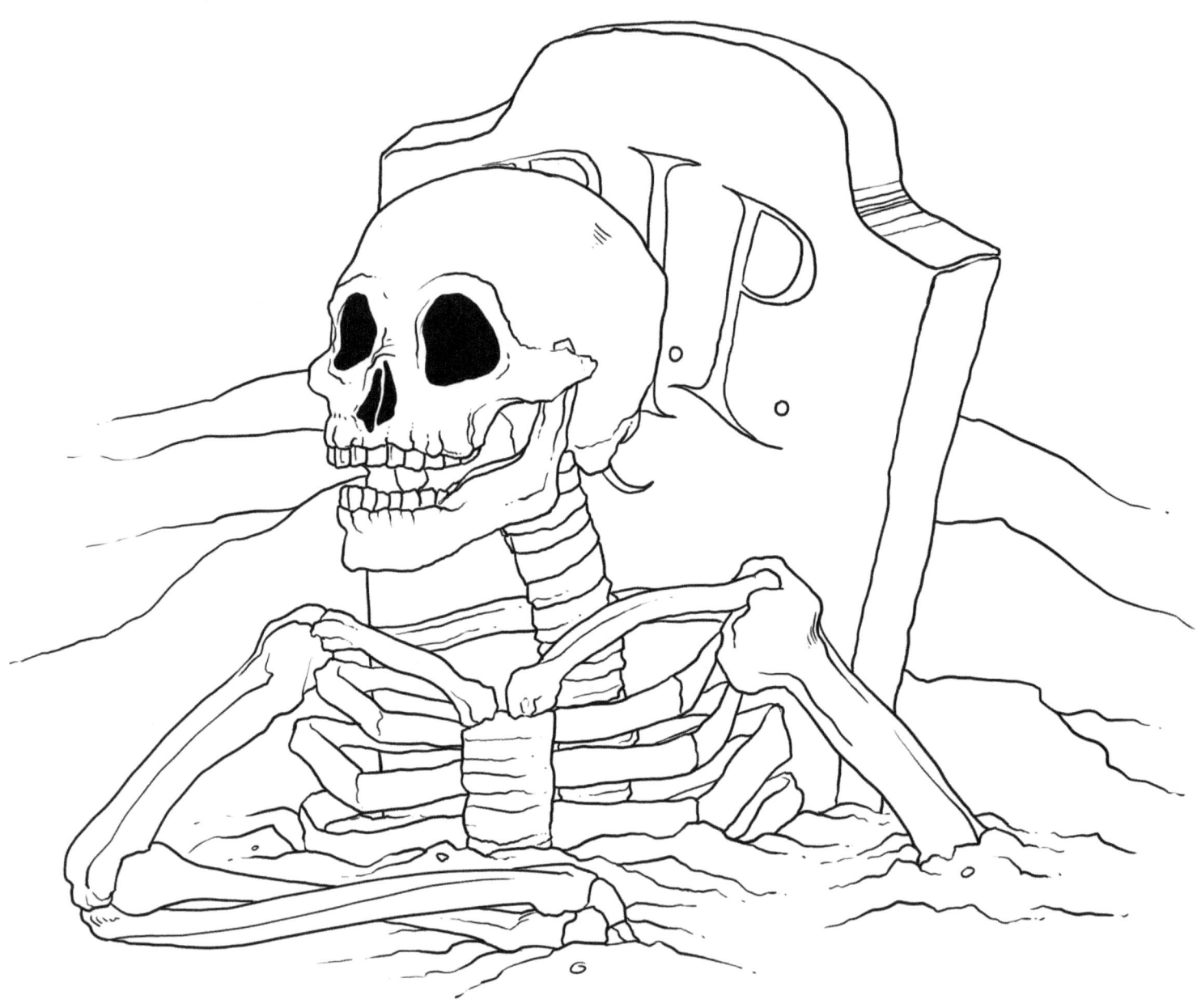

Thus believers try to convert everyone to Christianity so that the world can end and the resurrection of the dead can take place.

This Generation

Matthew 24:34 states, "Verily I say unto you, this generation shall not pass, till all these things be fulfilled."

Yet almost two thousand years have passed without Jesus returning to establish his kingdom on Earth.

Note that nowhere in the Old Testament prophesies do we find a suggestion that a messiah would need to come twice to impose divine will.

The Body of Christ

Catholics believe that priests have the power to change a wafer into the body of Christ.

Anyone who knows the correct incantation should be able to do it. But tell me, how would you know if you got the formula right?

Temptation

Lead us not into temptation,

but deliver us from evil.
Matthew 6:13

Changed Names

Names were changed to make Jesus, his parents and his brothers seem less Jewish.

HEBREW	ENGLISH	CHRISTIAN
Yeshua	Joshua	Jesus
Yosef	Joseph	Joseph
Miriam	Miriam	Mary
Yacov	Jacob	James
Yosef*	Joseph	Joses
Yudah	Judah	Juda
Shimon	Simon	Simon

*The oldest son usually is the one named after his father.

Unfortunately the gospels never provide the names of Jesus' sisters.
See Mark 6:3.

The Standard Jesus

Jesus usually is depicted as an Aryan looking man with blondish hair and beard.

Would he be remembered today if he had not been executed by Roman soldiers?
See John 19:23.

Studying Biology

Under the names creation science and intelligent design, the creation myth is used to challenge proven scientific explanations. Call it what you will, it's still that old time religion.

When the Old Testament Bible Got It Right!

Ecclesiastes 3:19 says, "For that which befalleth the sons of men befalleth beasts; even one thing befalleth them: as the one dieth, so dieth the other; yea, they have all one breath; so that a man hath no preeminence above a beast: for all is vanity."

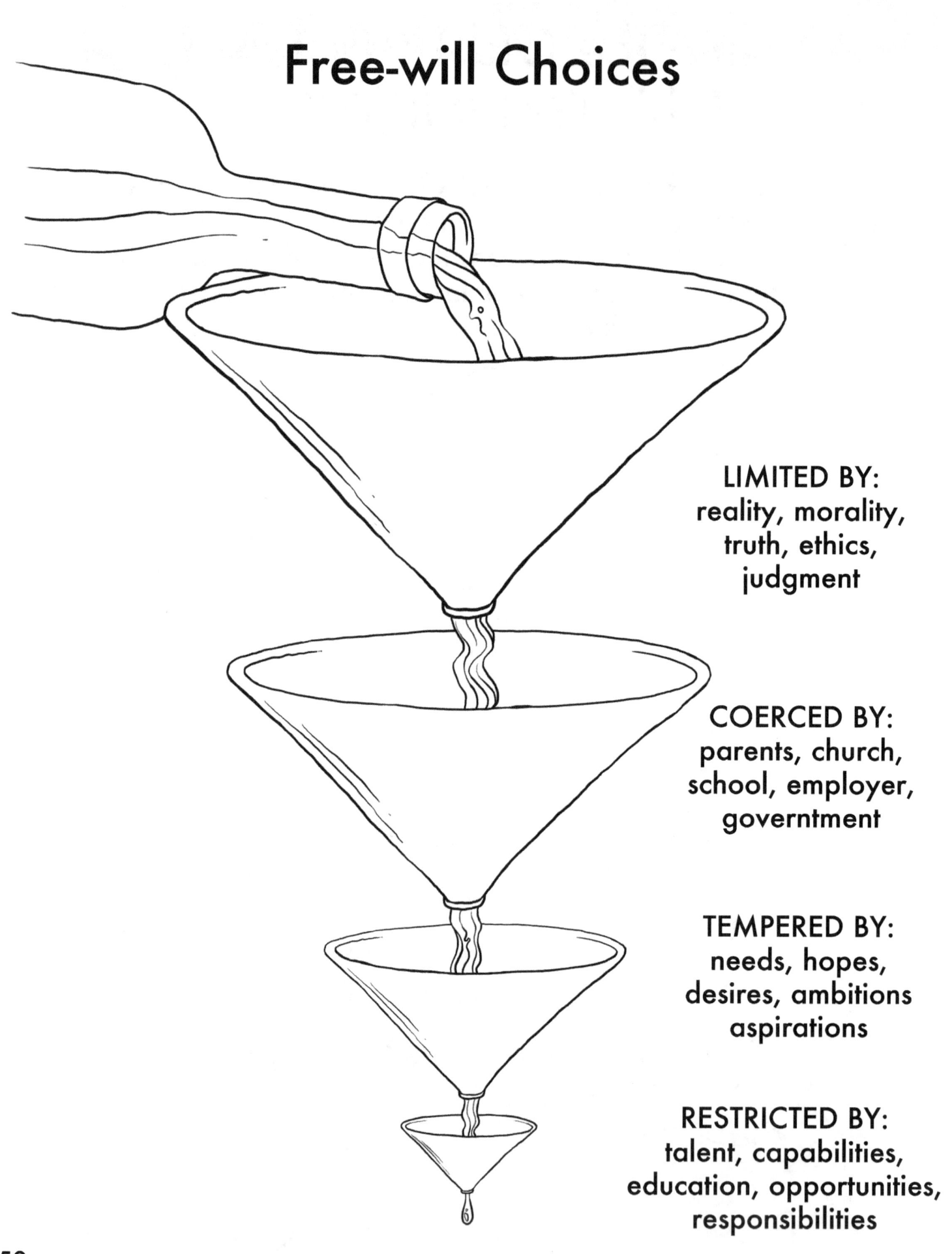

Pie in the Sky

Pleasure vs. Pain
Joy vs. Despair
Love vs. Hate
Acceptance vs. Rejection
Protection vs. Vulnerability
Triumph vs. Defeat
Forgiveness vs. Punishment
Justice vs. Suffering
Purification vs. Disease
Heaven vs. Death

Promises for bye and bye, when you die.

Off the Hook

God never is held responsible for any of life's misfortunes.

Instead the blame is heaped upon the victim if at all possible.

God's Good Deed

After being rescued by the helicopter he probably will credit God with the miracle that saved his life.

Why Everything Exists

Q: Why does everything exist?

A: Because God willed everything into existence.

Q: Why did God will everything into existence?

A: We cannot know the mind of God.

Q: Then how can you know that it was God who did it?

A: He is the only one capable of creating everything.

Q: What makes you so sure of that?

A: Otherwise he would not be God!

Using God as a default explanation only masks ignorance while removing any incentive to seek down-to-Earth anwers.

Arguing Back

The same arguments used by Creationists against Evolutionists can be turned around and used against them.
Take this example:

The Creationist says:
The Bible contains the truth about our origins.
Scientists have philosophically biased ways of thinking that prevent them from accepting the truth.

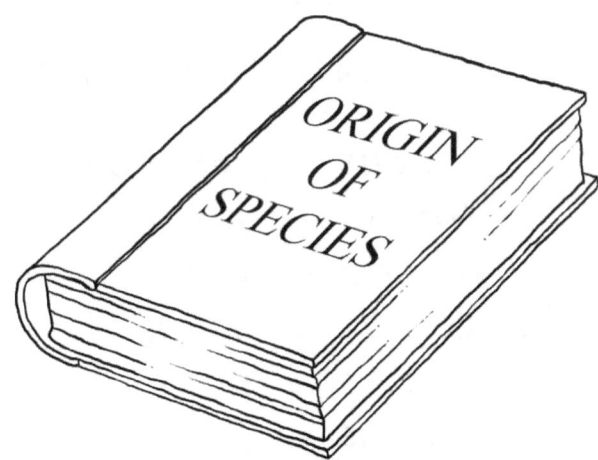

The Evolutionist says:
The Origin of Species contains the truth about our origins.
Believers have philosophically biased ways of thinking that prevent them from accepting the truth.

Not Much New Under the Sun

PAGAN   CHRISTIAN

Zeus = Jehovah
Apollo = Jesus
Athena = Mary
local gods = saints
oracles = popes
Vestal Virgins = priests
animal sacrifice = eucharist
Saturnalia = Christmas

Parallel Thinking

The Eleven Commandments

We think of the Ten Commandments as being more impressive than they really are. Many of the commandments no longer are observed, and none of them carry any penalty.

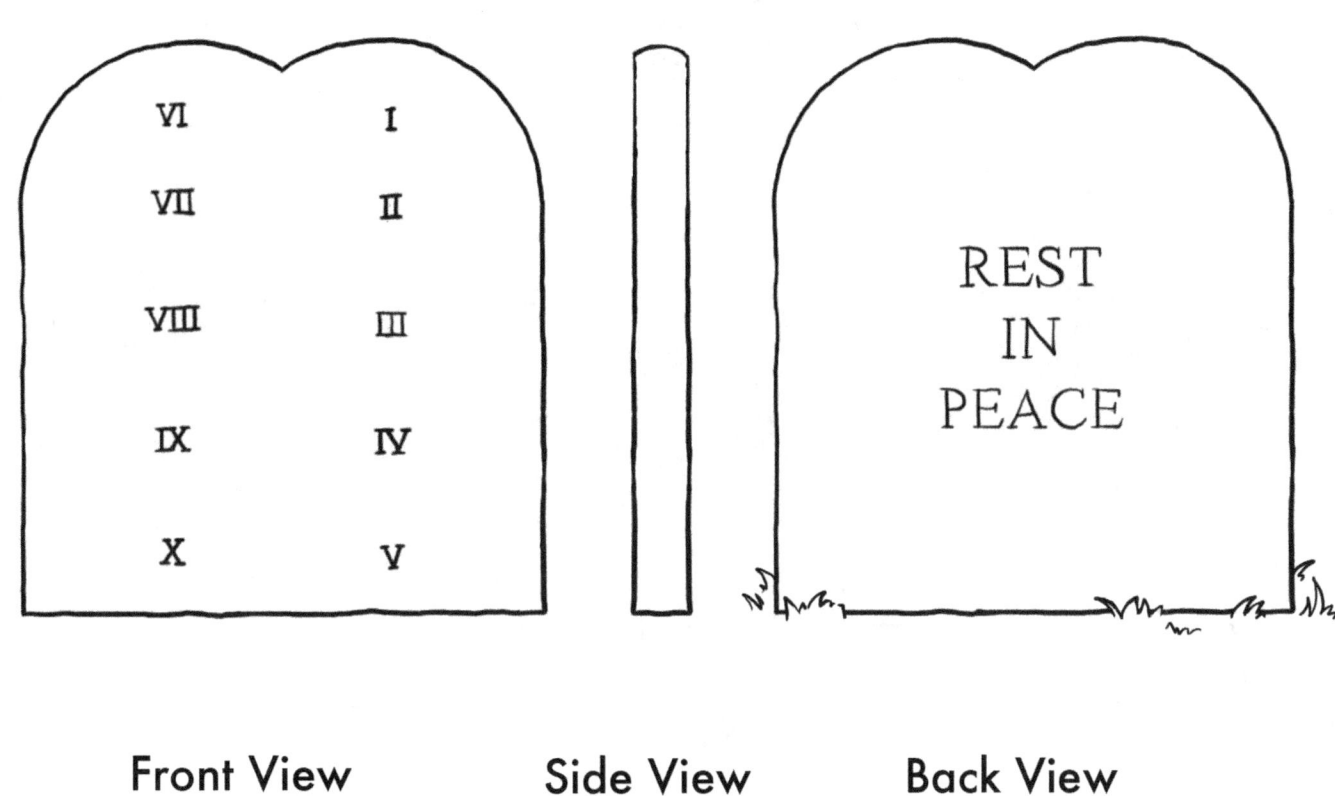

Front View   Side View   Back View

In John 13: 34-35 Jesus imposed an Eleventh Commandment, which is rarely if ever followed. "A new commandment I give unto you, That ye love one another; as I have loved you, that ye also love one another. By this shall all men know that ye are my disciples, if ye have love one to another."

How Do We Explain Everything?
Number 1

We are not obligated to explain anything as our ignorance does not imply that supernatural gods exist.

How Do We Explain Everything?

Everything is the result of cause and effect going back to the Big Bang.

What Caused the Big Bang?

As time started with the Big Bang, we cannot know what caused it.

Some "First Cause" Must Have Created the Big Bang.

Rather than an unseen but complex god, perhaps energy or matter, as in Einstein's simple equation, is eternal and self-existent.

$$E=mc^2$$

**Then it never needed to be created.
And that is good enough for most of us.**

Thermodynamics

The Second Law of Thermodynamics tells us that the arrow of time flies in only one direction:

toward dissolution and decay, not toward perfection and paradise.

Randomness (Entropy) Increases Over Time.

The ice cube melts and its molecules become scattered in the water.

As time runs in only one direction, we cannot reassemble the ice cube.

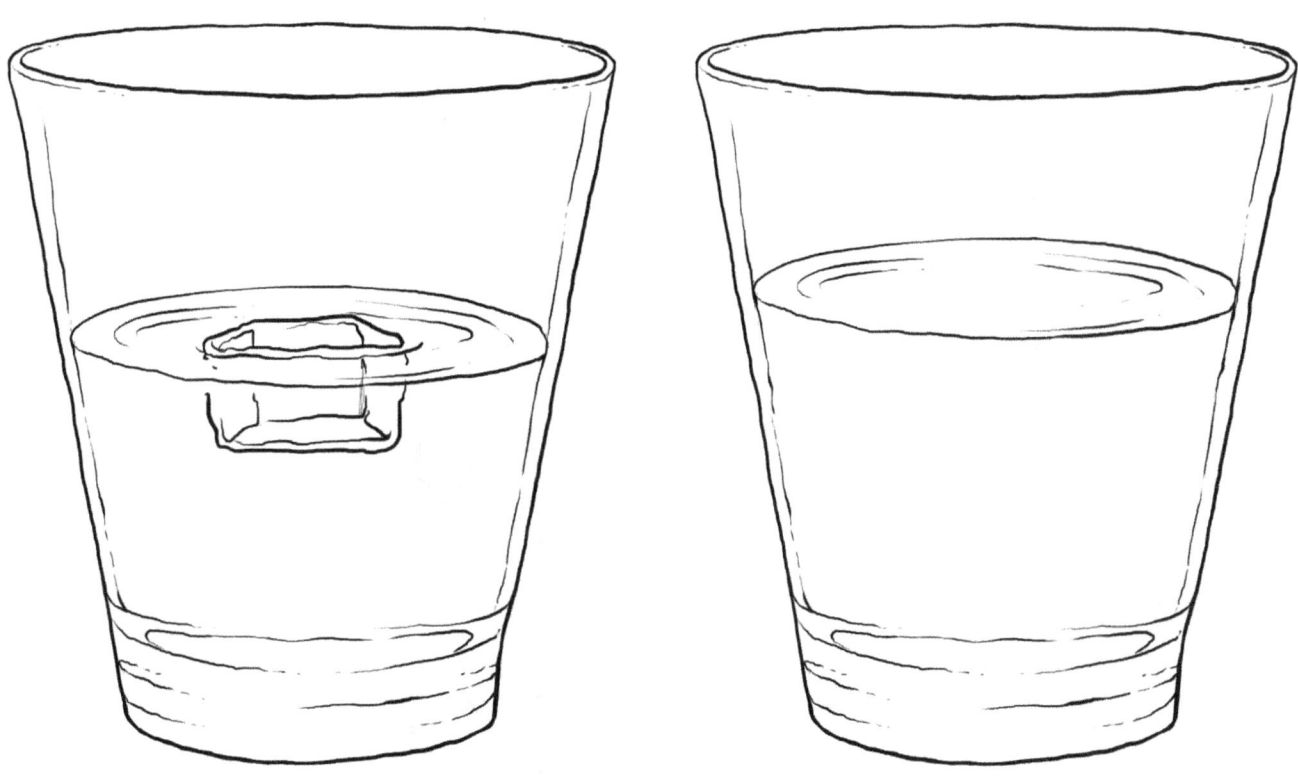

We cannot start over again in life or after we die.
Nature just does not work that way.

Open System

We do not live in a closed system as sunshine makes life on Earth possible. Without this constant source of energy plants and animals could not exist. We owe our life to energy from the Sun, not to the will of any god.

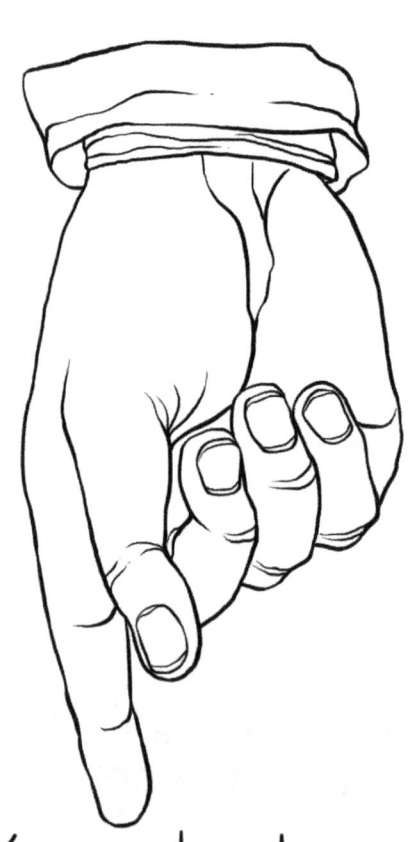

You are here!

The End

At death our existence ends forever. Only in biblical fiction are people revived days after they have died.

The end can come whether or not you have completed your coloring book, so go ahead and do it!

Activity: Atheist On Board

Let everyone know that we are on the move.

| ATHEIST ON BOARD | ATHEIST ON BOARD |

Color the background sky blue, or better yet, photocopy the page onto sky blue paper. Then you can cut out the sign and give one to every godless driver you know. It should be placed in the rear window.

Activity: Feed the Hungry.

Buy a few bags of inexpensive trail mix to give the needy.

If they say "God bless you." you can reply, "I am an Atheist, and I would rather be thanked by <u>you</u> than by some god."

Make a Mobile Part 1: Triple Trouble

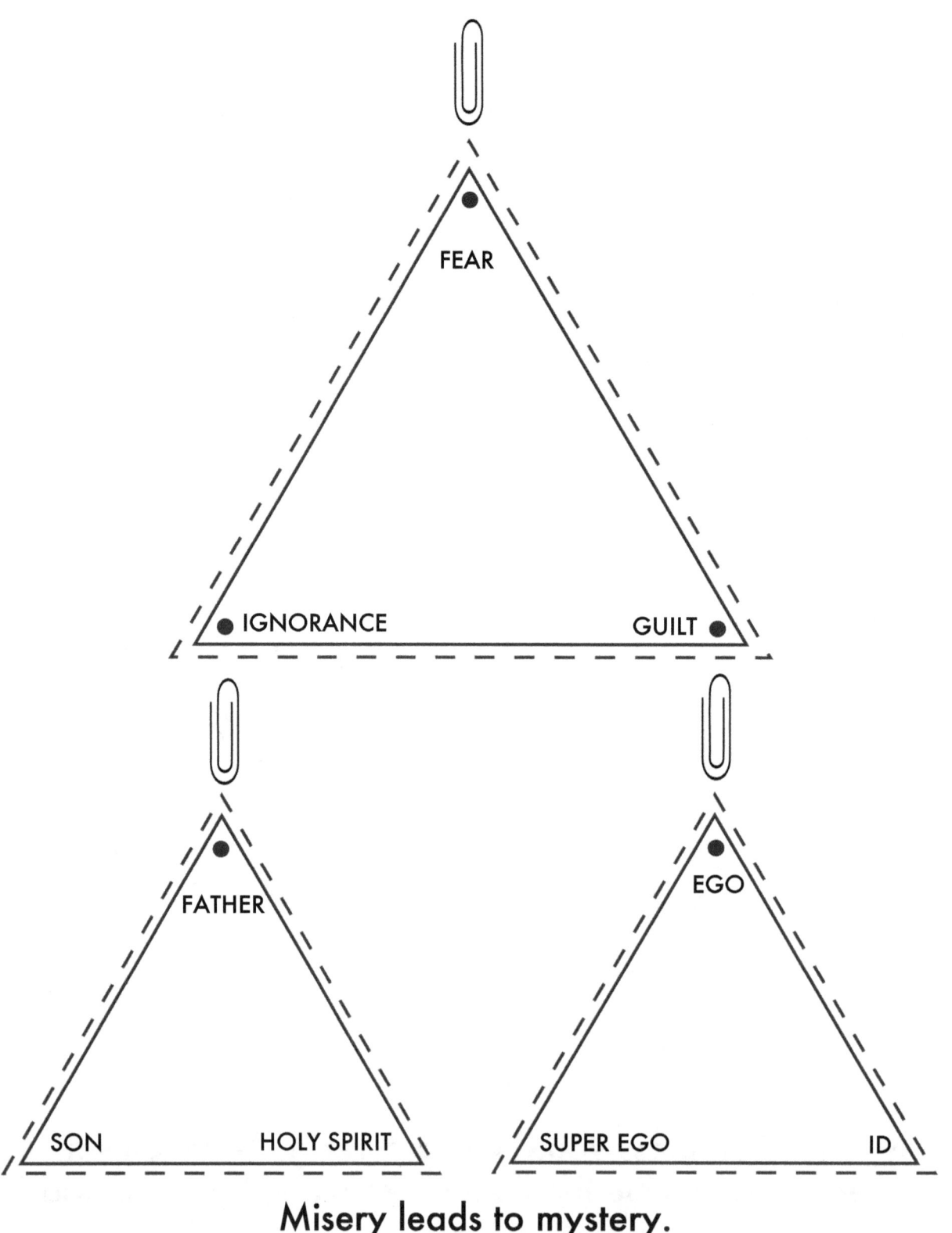

Misery leads to mystery.

Make a Mobile Part 2: Shining Stars

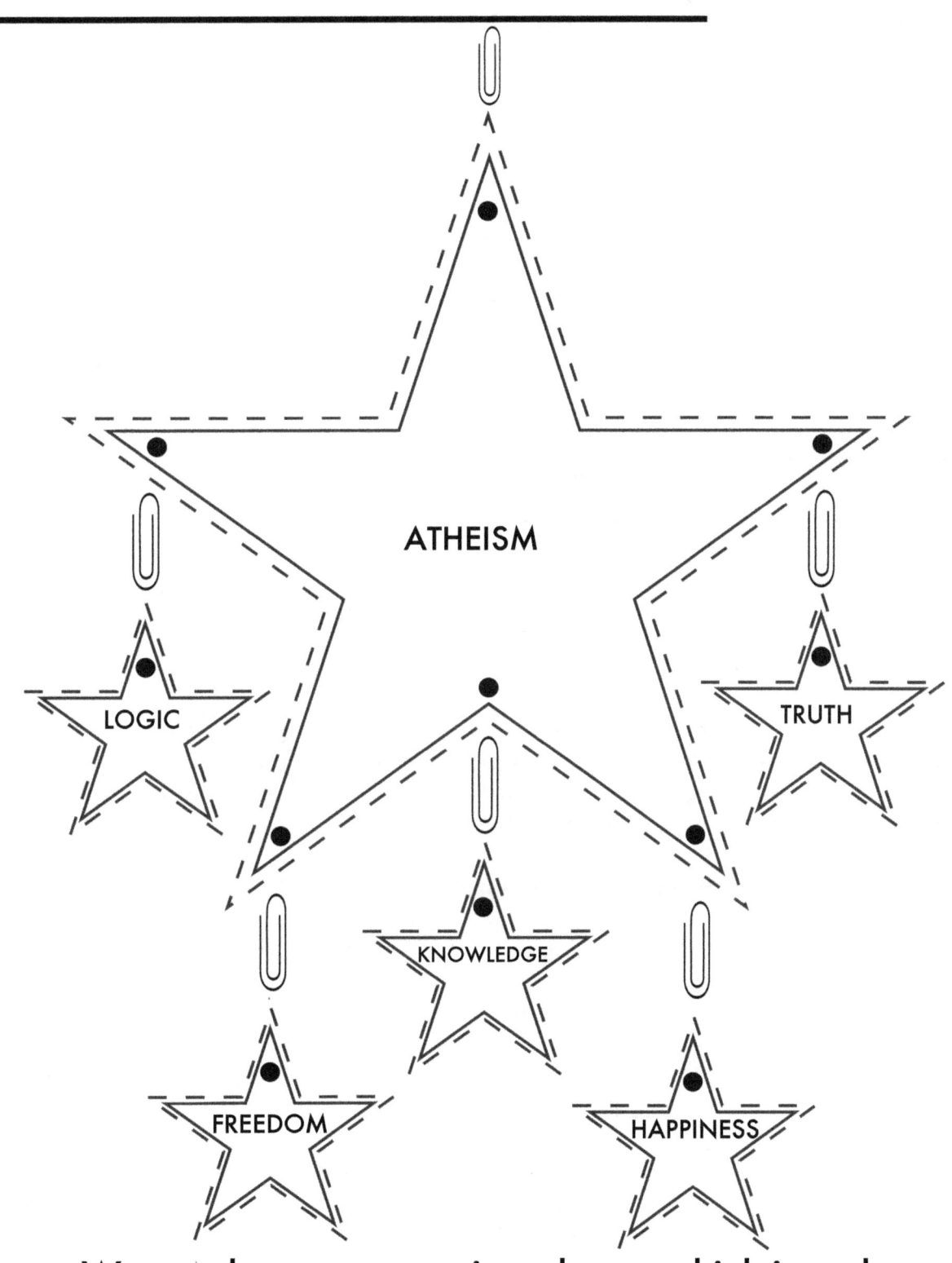

We need not compromise what we think in order to call ourselved "good" Atheists.

Activity: Change the Pledge.

Write your senators and representative in Congress at either their Washington or local addresses.

⎯⎯⎯⎯⎯⎯⎯⎯⎯⎯⎯⎯⎯⎯⎯⎯⎯⎯
(your complete address, street)

⎯⎯⎯⎯⎯⎯⎯⎯⎯⎯⎯⎯⎯⎯⎯⎯⎯⎯
(city)

⎯⎯⎯⎯⎯⎯⎯⎯⎯⎯⎯⎯⎯⎯⎯⎯⎯⎯
(date)

⎯⎯⎯⎯⎯⎯⎯⎯⎯⎯⎯⎯⎯⎯⎯⎯⎯⎯
(name of senator or representative)

⎯⎯⎯⎯⎯⎯⎯⎯⎯⎯⎯⎯⎯⎯⎯⎯⎯⎯
(address)

⎯⎯⎯⎯⎯⎯⎯⎯⎯⎯⎯⎯⎯⎯⎯⎯⎯⎯

Dear ⎯⎯⎯⎯⎯⎯⎯⎯⎯⎯⎯⎯⎯⎯:

Many of us do not believe in supernatural gods, but all good Americans believe in the rule of law. Therefore I propose that a slight change be made to the Pledge of Allegiance: that "one nation under the Constitution" be substituted for "one nation under God".

Such a minor change seems fair and equitable to all.

Thank you for considering this simple but reasonable suggestion.

Sincerely yours,

⎯⎯⎯⎯⎯⎯⎯⎯⎯⎯⎯⎯⎯⎯⎯⎯⎯⎯
(your signature)

⎯⎯⎯⎯⎯⎯⎯⎯⎯⎯⎯⎯⎯⎯⎯⎯⎯⎯
(your name printed)

Activity: BLAH, BLAH, BLAH

Has this book been nothing more than "preaching to the choir"?

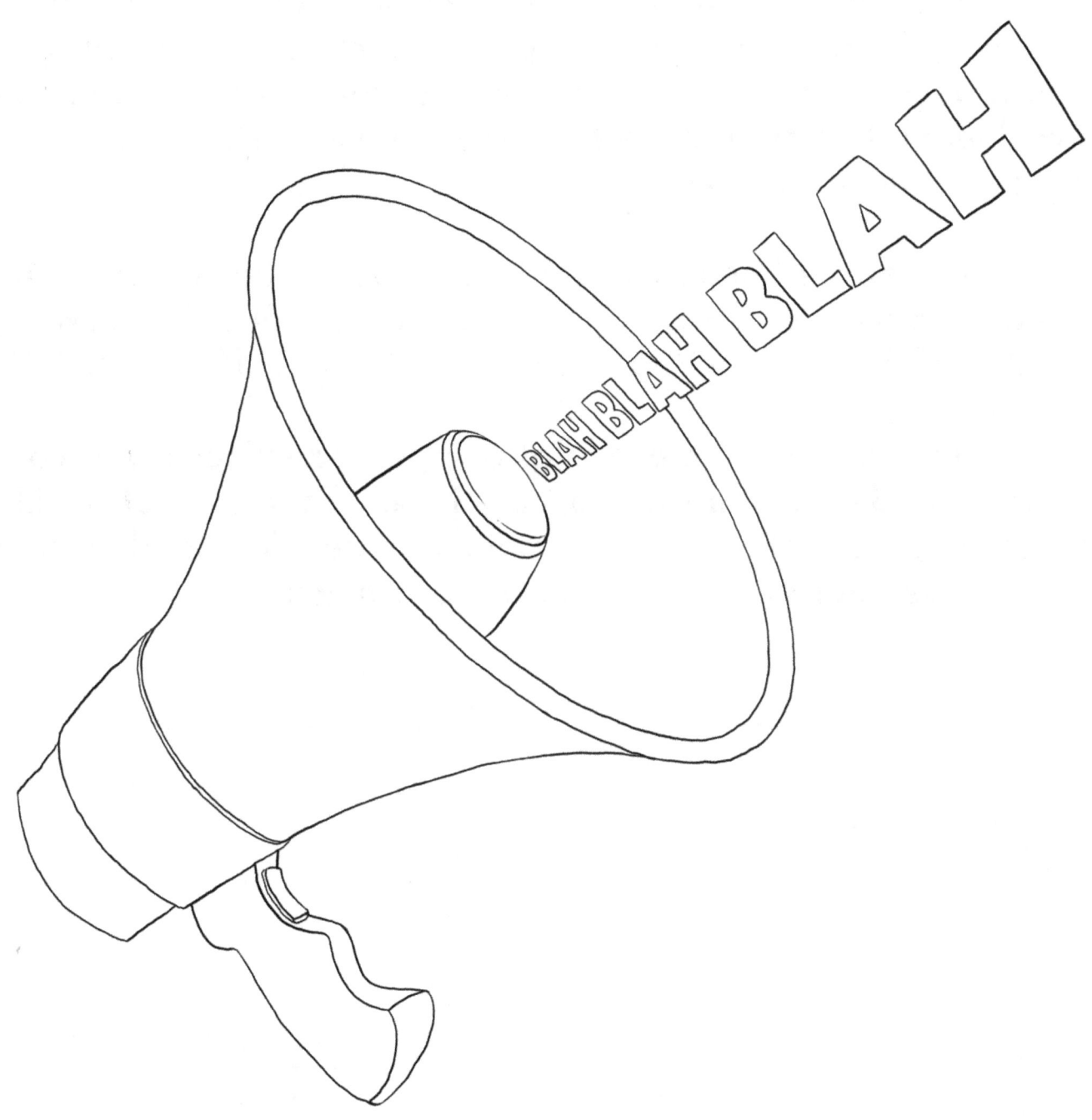

If you enjoyed coloring it, tell the publisher that you want more fun Atheist books, but most of all, give a copy to everyone on your list!

Activity: Get Involved.

Most Atheists are concerned about maintaining the separation of government and religion, but relatively few national organizations are fighting to keep the wall of separation intact. They need our support because the secular community is not as well organized or as well funded as are those who, for example, wish to teach religion in our public schools.

Therefore interested people should join organizations such as the Secular Coalition for America, 1012 14 Street NW, Washington, D.C. 20005-3429, suite 205, www.secular.org or (202)299-1091.

Most of all, we should be proud of being good citizens who vote for those candidates who support our issues. Then our votes will help to keep our nation secular, as the founders intended, and our voice will be heard in the councils of government.

Notes and Sketches

NEXT BIG THING BOOKS
7095 Hollywood Blvd.
Los Angeles, CA 90028

www.ingramcontent.com/pod-product-compliance
Lightning Source LLC
Chambersburg PA
CBHW060420300426
44111CB00018B/2922